Lee Canter's
Assertive Discipline®

Parent
Resource
Guide

Lee Canter and Marlene Canter
with
Barbara Schadlow

Lee Canter & Associates

© **1985 Lee Canter & Associates**

P.O. Box 2113, Santa Monica, CA 90407-2113

800-262-4347   310-395-3221

Printed in the United States of America

ISBN #09608978-7-9

First printing June 1985

97 96 95 94   13 12 11 10 9

Editorial Staff

Kathy Winberry

Susan Parker Lewis

Acknowledgement

This book would not exist without the professional dedication of both Barbara Schadlow and Kathy Winberry. They helped guide this project from its inception to its conclusion. Thanks to both of you.

A Message from Lee and Marlene Canter

Dear Parents:

You're about to plunge into a new and exciting way of relating to your child. You're about to make some very positive changes in your home. The vehicle that will assist you is the Assertive Discipline for Parents program. We invite you to step on board.

Our first book, **Assertive Discipline for Parents**, discusses in detail this new approach to parenting. In it you will learn how to acquire the take-charge attitude necessary to manage your child's behavior more effectively. You will also learn how to develop a plan for solving any behavior problems that arise in your home.

Our **Parent Resource Guide** was written because thousands of parents who attended our Workshops and read our first book said to us: "Help us be more consistent. Give us more ideas!" Responding to that request, we scanned the country for ideas that worked and put them together for you. Everything you need to develop a discipline plan and put it into action is right in your hands — practical ideas, **contracts** to fill out, **awards** to present to your child, **positive charts** to motivate your child to behave, and lots of **stickers** to make the process fun and exciting for the whole family.

This **Parent Resource Guide** is meant to be used. By that we mean you can write in it, dog-ear it, and tear out the pages you need. Keep it close at hand, and refer to it whenever you are looking for an idea, want to prevent a problem, or need to solve one.

As we said earlier, you're about to make some changes. We've given you the concepts. It's up to you to put them into action. You'll be on your way to success sooner than you could have imagined.

Sincerely,

Lee Canter
Marlene Canter

Table of Contents

How to Use this Book

The **Assertive Discipline Parent Resource Guide*** is designed to be a handy tool for parents who are having problems disciplining their children. It is not necessary to read it cover to cover. Rather, it is divided into the 10 most common problems areas parents face, so you can conveniently flip to the sections that are pertinent to situations that arise in your family. Though you may not use this book all at once, over the years you will find yourself referring to the various sections, when your children are young, and again when they are older. So keep it handy, within easy reach.

Each of the 10 chapters addresses a particular problem and takes you through the steps necessary to solve it. As you read, have pen in hand to jot down your course of action, and, if possible, work on the solutions with your spouse.

1. Pinpoint the Problem

Your first step in each chapter is to determine exactly what your child is doing that you want stopped. Check off the problem you are having or write it down in your own words in the space provided. **Remember To Be Specific**. Vague statements like "my child is bad" or "she's driving me crazy" will make it difficult for you to develop concrete solutions. More appropriate are phrases like "he pulls his sister's hair" or "she leaves her clothes on the floor every day."

2. Take Action

Your next step in each chapter will be to take some simple action to eliminate the problem. We suggest you NOT begin disciplining your child at this point. Instead take some time to think about what you, as a parent can do to help your child avoid undesirable behavior. One parent told us that the greatest problem in her home was that, "My children fight like cats and dogs when they sit down at the dinner table." We asked her to consider what she could do to prevent this nightly battle. After some thought she realized that the arguing always ended the moment dinner was served. She began calling her children to the table after the food was already at their places. This simple action on her part put an immediate end to what had been a very stressful situation.

In each chapter we offer many possibilities for eliminating problems. The ideas we believe are most important are indicated with a star (★). Check off the ones you will try, or write down your own ideas in the space provided.

*For further details on the concepts discussed in this book and a more complete explanation of the Assertive Discipline for Parents program, refer to **Assertive Discipline for Parents** (Canter and Associates, Inc., 1982.)

3. Develop an Assertive Discipline Plan

No doubt some of you are thinking, "A simple solution like that would never work with my child!" If, in fact, the action you have taken has not done the trick, and you find yourself caught in a constant power struggle, it is time to discipline your child. This is done by devising a simple Assertive Discipline Plan. There are three elements to such a plan — the **Rule**, the **Consequence** and the **Reward**. Each chapter gives you suggestions for developing a plan that suits your family.

The **Rule** you determine will evolve directly from the problem you pinpointed. For example, if your problem is getting your son to bed on time, the new rule in your home might be: "Brian must be in bed at 8 PM." In each chapter we list some of the rules that may be fitting for your family. Check the one you will use or devise your own and write it in the space provided.

A **Consequence** must be provided for your child if he or she does not follow your rule. Choose consequences that are appropriate for the age of your child and your particular family situation. Be sure to use consequences with which you are comfortable and that are neither physically nor psychologically harmful to your child. Check off any one of the suggested consequences in each chapter or come up with your own.

Next, you must **Reward** your child when he or she follows the rule. The key to a successful Assertive Discipline Plan is balancing negative consequences with positive reinforcement. When your child exhibits appropriate behavior, reward him or her with a special treat or privilege. Use any of the rewards we suggest, or determine a reward that is especially favored by your child. Aside from rewarding your child, you should frequently praise your child for following your rules.

4. Fill Out the Contract

Once the **Rule**, **Consequence** and **Reward** are determined, fill out the **Contract** at the end of the chapter and post it in a central location in your home (the refrigerator, a bulletin board, the bedroom door). The act of writing down your course of action and posting it will serve two important purposes. First, it will solidify the plan in your own mind and be a convenient reminder for you to be consistent. Second, the physical presence of your plan will send the message to your child that you are very serious about changing his or her behavior and that you have taken a great deal of time and effort to see that the changes are made.

5. Use the Positive Chart and Awards

Each chapter also contains a **Positive Chart**. These charts will become part of your **Reward** system and should also be posted. Whenever your child follows your rule, place one of the stickers found in this book on the chart. (To vary your reward system, use colorful markers, stars, or stamps, or purchase additional stickers that appeal to your child.) As soon as a predetermined number of stickers are placed on the chart, your child earns the reward. Younger children should earn their reward after two or three days; older children can wait a little longer, about a week.

The reward you choose may be a privilege, like staying up late, or a tangible item, like receiving tickets to a favorite movie. Some children can be motivated to behave with a special **Award** for good behavior. (Refer to the Glossary on pages 109-110 for an explanation of the difference between reward and award.) These awards are provided for your use in each chapter. One award on the page is for younger children, and one is for older children. Fill out the award and hang it in a place that all can see. These awards are also suitable for framing.

6. Put Your Plan into Action

When your plan is complete and your contract filled out, the next step is to discuss your Assertive Discipline Plan with your child. When everyone is calm, sit down with your family and clearly and firmly communicate your expectations.

For example, say something like: "Your dad and I are not happy with the way the two of you have been acting toward each other. We have come up with a way to put a stop to all of the fighting. We have written this contract." (Show contract.) "From now on the rule is: There is no fighting in this house. If either of you chooses to fight, you will go to bed right after dinner, no playing, no TV. On the other hand, when you spend 24 hours without a fight, we will place a sticker on this chart." (Show Sibling Chart.) "When the chart is filled, we will take you to the movies." Post the contract and the chart in a prominent place - on the refrigerator, on the wall, or on a door.

7. Be Consistent

Just laying out a plan and discussing it with your child will not guarantee success. For your plan to work, you must use it **consistently**. By consistently we mean **every single time** your child's behavior warrants it, you must follow through with the consequence you promised to use.

Being consistent isn't easy. There will be times when it may seem difficult to follow through with your plan. But remember that in order to make a long-lasting change in your child's behavior you must put every effort into backing up your words with action. By doing as you said you would, you are sending a very important message to your child: "I love you too much to allow you to misbehave. You mean so much to me that I will do everything necessary to help you improve your behavior."

Chapter 1

Following Directions

Following Directions

Chapter One

If you're like most parents, the greatest problem you probably face is that your child doesn't listen to you. You can tell your child to do something once, twice or three times, and your words seem to be completely ignored.

> "Laura, go brush your teeth." (Laura ignores you and continues to play.) "Laura, it's time to brush your teeth and get ready for bed." (Laura still ignores you.) "Laura, I don't want to say it again. Brush your teeth, NOW!"

Following directions is a problem that many parents encounter with their children frequently throughout the day. Though it can be worked on within the specific problem areas in this book, it is often prevalent in all situations. Therefore, we devote a separate section to it.

When working on this problem keep in mind the two most important reasons why you must teach your child to do as you say:

As a parent, you have the right to make reasonable requests of your child and feel assured that whatever you've requested will be carried out, not ignored or argued about.

Your child must learn to comply with the reasonable requests of the person in authority.

1. Pinpoint the Problem

Identify the specific way in which your child responds to your directions. Does your child:

____ Ignore you.

____ Say no.

____ Say yes, but not do it.

____ Take too long.

____ Argue with you.

____ Other _____

2. Take Action

Try some of these techniques to help you remain firm in stating your directions.

____ *Use an assertive approach when giving directions. Walk over to your child, look him or her straight in the eyes; then give your direction in a calm and determined voice. Don't get upset and don't sound angry. "Margo, I want you to put away your toys right now!"

____ Use the "broken-record" technique. Repeat your direction three times. If your child still doesn't listen, offer a consequence as a choice. Again, stay calm and speak softly, but firmly. The broken-record technique is an excellent verbal skill that can be used in many situations.

"Mark, stop jumping on the sofa." (Mark continues jumping.)
"Mark, I told you to stop jumping on the sofa." (Mark ignores you.)
"Mark, stop jumping on the sofa right now!" (Mark does not stop.)
"Mark, you have a choice. Either you stop jumping on the sofa or you will have to go to your room until dinner time."

____ Give a direction; then count to three. This is a favorite technique of many parents.

"Duane, tie your shoes. We have to go out." Duane continues playing. "Duane, I'm in a hurry. One…, two…."

____ Set a timer; then walk out of the room.

"Carol, pick up your toys. It's almost dinner time." Carol ignores her father. "Carol, I'm setting this timer for ten minutes, and I'm going inside to start dinner. When it rings, I expect to see all of your toys put away!"

____ Be selective in your directions. Try not to "nag" at your child all day long. (Do this. Do that.) You have a better chance of your directions being followed if they are well spaced throughout the day.

If the problem continues…

3. Develop an Assertive Discipline Plan

If the previous ideas are not successful, you will have to provide a consequence to your child for not listening to you. First state the **Rule**; then inform your child of the **Consequence** or **Reward** that will follow. Then fill out the **Contract** on the next page.

The Rule

The first rule in your house should be:

Follow directions the first time they are given.

The Consequence

What will you do if your child does not follow the rule? Your child will:

___ Lose a special privilege or activity.

___ Be grounded in his or her room for a designated period of time with no games, stereo, or telephone privileges. (older child)

___ Be placed in the "crabby chair" for a designated number of minutes. (younger child)

___ Other _____

The Reward

Be sure to praise your child when he or she begins to follow your directions. You may also reward your child in any of these ways.

Your child may:

___ Earn a sticker on the DIRECTIONS CHART. (See page 15.)

___ Be awarded the DIRECTIONS AWARD. (See page 17.)

___ Stay up later on an evening of your choice.

___ Receive special time with you.

___ Have a special evening with you at the library.

___ Other _____

Following Directions Contract

The new rule in our house will be:

_____

If _____
Child's Name

does not follow the rule,

_____
Consequence

If _____

does follow the rule,

_____
Reward

Date _____

GOOD LISTENING!

When I reach my goal of ____ stickers,
I will earn _____

Parents: First determine the goal and reward, then place a sticker on the chart whenever your child follows directions. Younger children earn the reward in a few days, older children in a week.

Good Listening

This award is presented to

_____

for

_____

Date _____

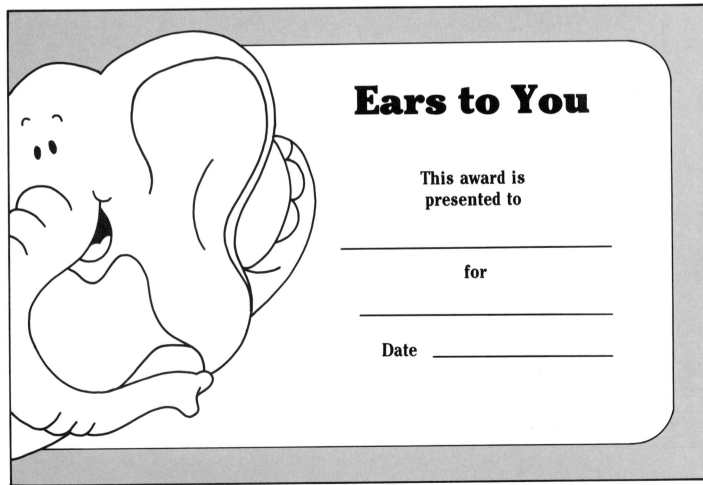

Ears to You

**This award is
presented to**

_____

for

_____

Date _____

Chapter 2

Verbal Problems

Verbal Problems

Chapter Two

The two most important reasons for teaching your child how to communicate properly are:

Your child must learn that there are socially acceptable and appropriate ways of asking for what he or she wants.

It can be very annoying to be around a child who whines, cries or argues.

1. Pinpoint the Problem

Identify the specific verbal problem you are having. Does your child:

___ Interrupt your conversations.

___ Whine to get his or her way.

___ Talk back or argue.

___ Curse.

___ Other _____

2. Take Action

Verbal problems usually occur when a child can't get his or her way. The child will cry, whine, argue or shout in an attempt to coax you to give in to his or her demands. It is important to teach your child that he or she won't get what's wanted by being verbally abusive. The child must learn to communicate wishes in a normal tone of voice; then accept whatever decision you, the adult, consider appropriate. Here are some ideas.

Which ones will you try?

___ *Explain to your child exactly how you expect him or her to communicate what is wanted.

___ *Be sure to give your child plenty of attention and positive reinforcement when he or she speaks appropriately.

___ Teach your child the proper words or use role play to show methods of expression. (What to say and do when company comes. How to ask parents for something.)

___ Give feedback when your child whines, cries, etc. ("You're whining again.")

___ Prepare your child before entering a situation where verbal problems may occur.

"Nicki, I'm going to be on the phone for the next 10 minutes. I don't want you to interrupt me. Let's find something for you to do," or "Robby, my friend is going to visit me today. I want you to play by yourself while we talk. Let's take some of your toys off the shelf so you can keep busy."

___ If your child is unrelenting in his or her demands, try to ignore the whining or yelling. If it really gets to you, turn on a radio or walk out of the room.

___ If your child curses, clearly state your expectations. ("Scott, I don't want to hear you using those words ever again.") If the cursing continues, provide your child with a consequence.

___ Tape record your child's voice so he or she can hear the yelling, whining, or cursing.

___ Do not give into a child who yells his or her demands. Explain that you will only do what your child wants if he or she speaks appropriately.

___ Other _____

If the problem continues...

3. Develop an Assertive Discipline Plan

If teaching your child how to communicate hasn't worked, you will need to take stronger action and use an Assertive Discipline Plan. Determine the **Rule**, **Consequence** and **Reward**; then fill out the **Contract** on the next page.

The Rule

What will be the new rule in your house? Your child will:

____ Refrain from interrupting when you're talking to someone.

____ Refrain from whining when he or she wants something.

____ Refrain from arguing or talking back to you.

____ Refrain from cursing.

____ Other _____

The Consequence

Decide which consequence you will provide if your child continues to use inappropriate language. Your child will:

____ Be sent to his or her room to calm down.

____ Be isolated or placed in the "crabby chair" until proper language is used.

____ Be sent to bed five minutes earlier for every time the rule is broken. (Place a tally mark on a chart every time your child uses inappropriate language.)

____ Absolutely not get what he or she is asking for.

____ Other _____

The Reward

How will you reward your child for following the rule. Your child may:

____ Earn a sticker on the chart on page 25.

____ Be given the award on page 27.

____ Get a kiss from you every time he or she catches himself or herself using inappropriate language and changes the words or tone quickly.

____ Have a special treat the first time he or she doesn't interrupt your conversation. (younger child)

____ Buy a new record for spending one week without using any inappropriate four-letter words. (older child)

____ Other _____

Verbal Problems Contract

The new rule in our house will be:

_____

If _____
Child's Name

does not follow the rule,

_____
Consequence

If _____

does follow the rule,

_____
Reward

Date _____

Sounds Great!

When I reach my goal of _____ stickers, I will earn _____.

Parents: Whenever your child communicates in an appropriate manner, place a sticker on the chart. Younger children earn the reward in a few days, older children in a week.

Super Job

This award is presented to

_____

for

_____

Date _____

Something to Crow About

This award is presented to

_____

for

_____

Date_____

Chapter 3

Household Responsibilities

Household Responsibilities

Chapter Three

When working on this problem remember the two basic reasons why your child needs to be given responsibilities at home:

Today's busy families cannot function smoothly without everyone pitching in and doing their part.

A child needs to be given chores to develop into a responsible, self-reliant adult.

1. Pinpoint the Problem

Think about the specific chore or chores that present a problem; then identify the exact nature of the problem. Does your child:

____ Refuse to do chores at all.

____ Refuse to do chores on time.

____ Refuse to do chores according to your standards.

____ Complain about doing chores.

____ Need to be reminded to do chores.

____ Other _____

2. Take Action

The key to teaching responsibility is developing routines. Doing the same thing at the same time each day forms a habit that can easily be performed without much thought. Here are some ideas to encourage your child to assume more responsibility at home.

Check off the ones you will try.

____ *List everyone's name and chores on a chart. Schedule a day and time that each chore must be done.

____ *Be sure to go through the routine of doing the chore with your child so that he or she knows exactly what you expect.

____ Prepare a checklist for your child with the steps necessary for completing the chore correctly.

____ Have a family meeting to decide which family member should do each chore.

____ Pin a photograph of each family member next to his or her chore for the week. Rotate the photos weekly.

____ Have a grab bag. Write each chore on a separate piece of paper and place them in a paper sack. Each family member takes a turn grabbing into the bag until all the chores are chosen. Family members are free to exchange chores with one another if they wish.

____ Give your child verbal reminders or leave notes. (Tape a note to the bedroom door that reads, "Please clean your room today" or a note to the front door saying "Start the laundry after school.")

____ Teach your child how to make a personal time schedule.

Tommy's Day

3:15-3:30 rake lawn	4:30-4:45 set table	5:00-5:30 play or read
3:30-4:30 do homework	4:45-5:00 walk dog	

____ Purchase calendars or appointment books to help your child to schedule responsibilities on appropriate days. (What day to clean room, iron clothes, change linens, babysit)

____ Other _____

3. Develop an Assertive Discipline Plan

If the "Take Action" ideas don't work, use a simple Assertive Discipline Plan to teach your child responsibility. Decide the **Rule**, **Consequence** and **Reward**; then fill out the **contract** on page 33.

If the problem continues...

The Rule

What will be the new rule in your house? Your child will:

____ Do assigned chores.

____ Do chores on time.

____ Do chores according to your standards.

____ Do chores without complaining.

____ Do chores without being reminded.

____ Other _____

The Consequence

Utilize natural consequences whenever possible (if your son doesn't set the table, don't serve him dinner; if your daughter doesn't iron her clothes, don't do it for her). Also effective is to postpone a special activity until the chore is done, or take away a privilege for a specified time. ("Until you clean up your room, you may not ride your bike with your friends.") If your child breaks the rule, what privilege or activity will you take away as a consequence? Your child will:

____ Lose TV privileges.

____ Lose phone privileges.

____ Lose the privilege of playing outside with friends.

____ Lose after-school sports participation privileges.

____ Lose an allowance or receive less allowance.

____ Do one of your chores TWO times.

____ Other _____

Tip: When your child refuses to pick up his or her toys or clothes: put them in a box or laundry basket and store them out of reach for one week, or pile the items on your child's bed, thereby preventing him or her from going to sleep until everything is put away.

The Reward

How will you reward your child for following the rule? Your child may:

____ Earn a sticker on the CHORE CHART. (See page 35.)

____ Be awarded the CHORE AWARD. (See page 37.)

____ Have you do one of his or her chores.

____ "Rest" on the 7th day if all chores were finished each day for 6 days.

____ Stay up later on the weekend if all chores were completed Monday through Friday.

____ Have a friend stay overnight.

____ Other _____

Chore Contract

The new rule in our house will be:

_____

If _____
Child's Name

does not follow the rule,

_____
Consequence

If _____

does follow the rule,

_____
Reward

Date_____

Household Responsibilities Chart

I Service Schedule I

When I reach my goal of _____ stickers, I will earn _____

Parents: Younger children receive one sticker for each chore completed according to the rules. Older children receive one sticker for each day that all chores are completed according to the rules.

You Did It!

This award is presented to

_____

for _____

Date _____

Super Duper Job!

This award is presented to

_____

for _____

Date _____

Chapter 4

Morning Routine

Morning Routine

Chapter Four

When working on this problem, keep in mind the three most important reasons why your child must have a well-defined morning routine:

▓▓▓Without routine, mornings become hectic and it is difficult for your family to get to school and work on time.

▓▓▓You have a right to have your child cooperate in the morning.

▓▓▓A peaceful morning sets the tone for the rest of the day.

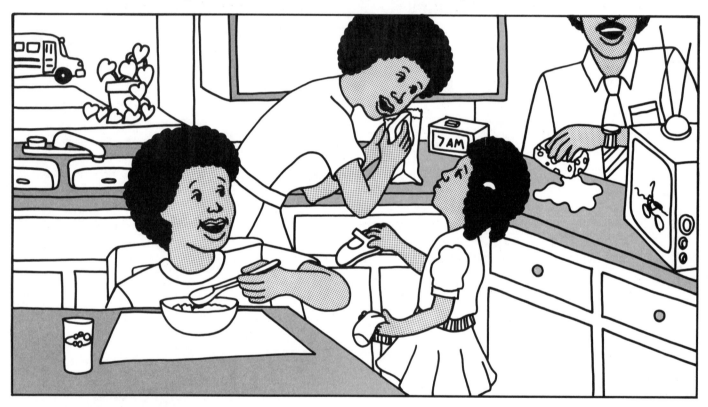

1. Pinpoint the Problem

Identify the specific problem that occurs in the morning. Does your child:

___ Get up too late.

___ Need help getting dressed.

___ Get to breakfast late.

___ Fight with siblings for use of the bathroom.

___ Leave the bedroom a mess.

___ Miss the bus or keep the carpool waiting.

___ Spend too much time watching TV.

___ Have trouble gathering his or her belongings.

___ Other _____

2. Take Action

Now, think about what you can do to guide your family toward developing a peaceful morning routine. Does everyone have a specific time to wake up, to be washed and dressed, to be eating breakfast? If they are old enough, do your children share in the morning reponsibilities? Do they make their own beds or make their own lunches? Here are some ideas. Which ones will you try?

___★At a family meeting discuss the new routines and responsibilities.

___★Write down the morning schedule and post it for all to see.

___ Give your child an alarm clock and teach him or her how to use it.

___ Wake your child; then set a timer to ring when he or she must be up and dressed.

___ Have your older child lay out his or her clothes the night before school.

___ Discuss the night before what your child will wear to school.

___ Make lunches the night before school, or give your child that responsibility.

___ Develop a time schedule for bathroom use. For example,
Steve 7:15 - 7:30, Ellen 7:30 - 7:45, Jerry 7:45 - 8:00

___ Make a list of chores and check off each chore as it is completed. For example,

	Make bed	Feed dog	Clean dishes
Steve			
Ellen			
Jerry			

___ Place a box by the door in which your child can place belongings that must be taken to school (books, lunch, homework, jacket).

___ Give a 10-minute warning before the bus or carpool is expected.

___ Other _____

3. Develop an Assertive Discipline Plan

If your new routine hasn't solved the problem, it is time to develop an Assertive Discipline Plan. First determine the **Rule**, **Consequence** and **Reward**; then fill out the **Contract** and communicate the plan to your child.

If the problem continues…

The Rule

What will be the new rule in your house? Your child will:

____ Get up on time.

____ Get washed, dressed and ready for school without help.

____ Set aside enough time for breakfast.

____ Spend the morning without fighting with siblings.

____ Clean up room.

____ Be ready when the carpool or bus arrives.

____ Watch TV only when completely ready.

____ Gather belongings for school (lunch, homework, books).

____ Other _____

The Consequence

Use one of the following consequences, or choose your own. Your child will:

____ Go to his or her room after school for as many minutes as he or she was late getting out of bed in the morning.

____ Be served breakfast only after appearing at the table washed, dressed and ready for school.

> **Tip:** Use natural consequences whenever possible. If your child forgets to bring lunch money or homework to school, don't deliver it to him or her. Your child must learn the results of being irresponsible.

____ Wash the dishes if he or she arrives late at the breakfast table.

____ Lose the privilege of participating in an after-school activity.

____ Lose the privilege of playing with friends after school.

____ Stay in his or her bedroom until completely dressed.

____ Other _____

The Reward

How will you reward your child for following the rule? Your child may:

____ Earn a sticker on the MORNING CHART. (See page 45.)

____ Be awarded the MORNING AWARD. (See page 47.)

____ Participate in a special activity after school.

____ Choose breakfast for everyone if he or she is the first one to be seated at the table.

____ Have a "special dress day" to wear whatever he or she wants.

____ Watch morning TV until it's time to leave if he or she gets ready quickly.

____ Other _____

Morning Contract

The new rule in our house will be:

_____

If _____
Child's Name

does not follow the rule,

_____
Consequence

If _____

does follow the rule,

_____
Reward

Date _____

Morning Routine Chart

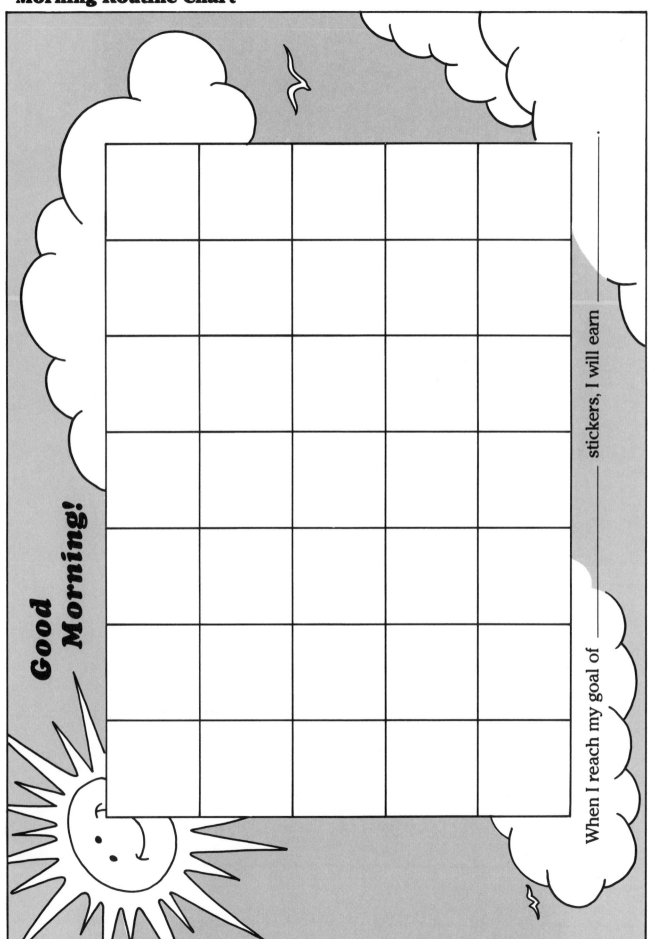

Good Morning!

stickers, I will earn _____.

When I reach my goal of _____

Parents: Every morning that your child behaves, place a sticker on the chart. Younger children earn the reward in a few days, older children in one week. A special reward may also be earned after receiving a specified number of stickers in a month.

Record Breaking Morning Award

presented to

_____

for

_____

Date _____

You Beat the Clock Award

presented to

_____

for

_____

Date_____

Chapter 5

Sibling Rivalry

Sibling Rivalry

Chapter Five

When working on this problem, keep in mind the three most important reasons for helping your children solve the problems they have relating to their brothers and sisters.

In order to promote harmony in your household and preserve your sanity, your children must learn to get along with each other (even if it's merely peaceful coexistence).

Working out problems with siblings will be a child's first step in learning to get along with people.

Today's busy parents have precious little time with their children. That time can be spent on better things than mediating battles between siblings.

1. Pinpoint the Problem

Identify the specific problem that occurs with your children. Do they:

___ Fight.	___ Have difficulty sharing.
___ Argue.	___ Tattle.
___ Tease.	___ Other _____
___ Play rough.	

2. Take Action

If your children are old enough, it is advisable to stay out of their arguments as long as you can, giving them the opportunity to solve the problem themselves. However, you should definitely intervene when necessary. Here are some ideas for dealing with this problem. Which ones will you try?

____ * Before your children begin to play, sit down with them and discuss how you expect them to behave with each other.

____ * Since boredom may lead to arguing or fighting, when your children are together be sure they have an activity to keep them busy.

____ If sharing is a problem, prepare a time schedule or set a timer to indicate when your children should take turns.

____ Allow each child to select one or two toys that are very special to him or her and need NOT be shared with siblings.

____ If the arguing is annoying to you, leave the room and busy yourself in another part of the house.

____ If tattling is a problem, ask your child to tell you two good things about his or her sibling before saying anything bad.

____ Draw names to determine who goes first in an activity, who chooses dinner, who selects the TV station.

____ To avoid fights, teach your children to communicate verbally to each other what is bothering them.

____ To prevent children from vying for your attention, spend separate time with each child to show them how important they both are to you.

____ Other _____

> Each day find at least three things your children do well and let them know you like it. Praise is the key to changing your child's behavior.

If the problem continues...

3. Develop an Assertive Discipline Plan

If the foregoing ideas do not work, it is time to develop an Assertive Discipline Plan. Determine the **Rule**, **Consequence** and **Reward**; then fill out the **Contract** on the next page.

The Rule

What will be the new rule in your house? Your children will:

____ Get along with each other without fighting or arguing.

____ Refrain from teasing each other.

____ Play calmly with each other.

____ Share their things.

____ Refrain from tattling on each other.

____ Other _____

The Consequence

As part of your Assertive Discipline Plan for sibling rivalry use one of the following consequences or choose your own. Your children will:

____ Be sent to separate parts of the house to "cool down."

____ Lose the privilege of playing games together for a specified time period.

____ Lose the privilege of participating in a family outing.

____ Not be allowed to play with the toy or game in question. (Keep the item in your closet for one week.)

____ Other _____

The Reward

The best way to motivate your children to get along with one another is to use "Marble Mania." (See chart, page 55.) Set a goal that both children can work toward and place a sticker on the chart whenever they behave. Your children can earn:

____ Tickets to the movies, ball game, a concert.

____ A "carte blanche" trip to the toy store.

____ An evening at the library or another "night out" with you.

____ The rental of a special video cassette.

____ Special time with you on an individual basis.

____ Other _____

Sibling Contract

The new rule in our house will be:

_____

If _____
Child's Name

does not follow the rule,

_____
Consequence

If _____

does follow the rule,

_____
Reward

Date _____

Fill It Up!

When we reach our goal of _____ stickers, we will earn _____.

Parents: Each time your children get along with each other, place a sticker on the chart.

SUPER KIDS AWARD

presented to

_____

for

_____

Date _____

TERRIFIC TEAMWORK AWARD

presented to

_____

for

_____

Date _____

Chapter 6

Mealtime

Mealtime

When working on this problem, keep in mind the following reasons for making mealtime (particularly dinner) pleasant for the whole family.

　It may be the first time of the day that the family can sit together and share the events of the day.

　You probably spent a great deal of time planning and preparing the meal.

　The whole family will enjoy their meal and each other better when the atmosphere is calm.

1. Pinpoint the Problem

Identify the specific problem that occurs during mealtime. Does your child:

____ Arrive late at the dinner table.

____ Laugh or act silly.

____ Fight with siblings.

____ Complain about the food you prepared.

____ Play with the food.

____ Refuse to clean up.

____ Talk too much and too loudly.

____ Get up and down from the table.

____ Other _____

2. Take Action

Here are some simple ideas that you can use to alleviate the most common problems during mealtime. Which ones will you try?

___ *Communicate your expectations to your child concerning appropriate behavior at the table.

___ *Separate siblings who don't get along at the table.

___ *Include your child in the conversation.

___ Assign a permanent seat at every meal.

___ Call your child to the table AFTER the meal is completely prepared and ready to be served.

___ When your child dawdles over the food, set a kitchen timer and remove the food when the bell rings.

___ Find out what your child's favorite foods are and plan to serve those foods periodically.

___ Hold a contest to see who is the quietest, who is the neatest, or who arrives first at the table. Present the winner with a reward.

___ Assign weekly responsibilities such as setting the table, clearing the table, and doing the dishes.

___ Turn off the TV during dinner to avoid distractions. Play pleasant music instead.

___ Other _____

> When using a discipline plan remember this: your child's behavior will change if you consistently provide consequences and rewards. Don't back down from your consequences. If you say it, do it!

If the problem continues...

3. Develop an Assertive Discipline Plan

If your child continues to cause problems at mealtime, then you must lay down the law. Determine the **Rule**, **Consequence** and **Reward**; then fill out the **Contract** on the next page and communicate the plan to your child.

The Rule

What will be the new rule in your house? Your child will:

____ Arrive at the table as soon as dinner is announced.

____ Eat without laughing or acting silly.

____ Eat without fighting at the table.

____ Eat without complaining about the meal.

____ Eat without playing with the food.

____ Clean up after eating.

____ Eat without yelling at the table.

____ Ask permission to leave the table.

____ Other _____

The Consequence

Choose one of the following consequences or use your own.

Your child will:

____ Be removed from the table.

____ Clear the table and wash the dishes.

____ Lose the privilege of playing outside after dinner.

____ Lose the privilege of watching TV after dinner.

____ Prepare his or her own meals for two days. (Older child)

____ Eat dinner alone for two days.

____ Other _____

The Reward

Remember, for change to take place, you must frequently praise and reward your child for positive behavior.

How will you reward your child for behaving during mealtime? Your child may:

____ Earn a sticker on the MEALTIME CHART. (See page 65.)

____ Be awarded a MEALTIME AWARD. (See page 67.)

____ Choose tomorrow's meal.

____ Spend time cooking a favorite dish.

____ Get a special dessert the next day.

____ Have a friend over for dinner.

____ Stay up later on an evening of your choosing.

____ Other _____

Mealtime Contract

The new rule in our house will be:

_____

If _____
Child's Name

does not follow the rule,

_____
Consequence

If _____

does follow the rule,

_____
Reward

Date _____

BIG DEAL MEAL

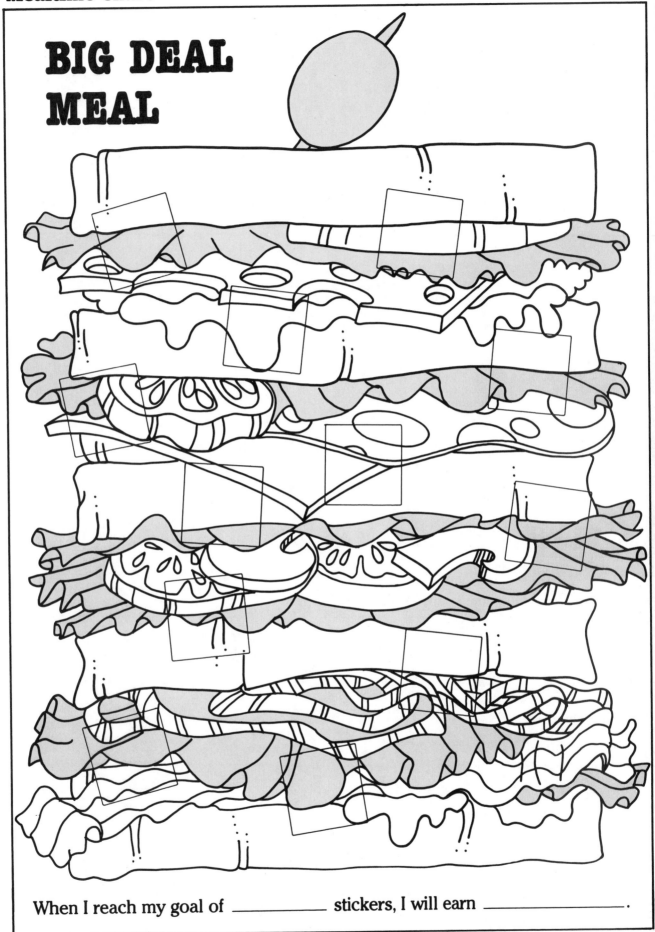

When I reach my goal of _____ stickers, I will earn _____.

Parents: When your child behaves according to the mealtime rule, place a sticker on the chart. Younger children earn the reward in a few days, older children in a week.

BIG DEAL MEAL AWARD

presented to

_____

for

_____

Date _____

Hot Dog

This award is presented to

_____

for _____

Date _____

Chapter 7

Bedtime Routine

Bedtime Routine

When working on this problem, keep in mind the three most important reasons why a child should be in bed on time:

Sleep is essential for a growing child — whether he or she wants it or not!

Parents, you need time alone in the evening. After a busy day you deserve some time for yourself or to be with your spouse.

A regular bedtime routine will enable the family to function more smoothly the next morning.

1. Pinpoint the Problem

Identify the specific problem that occurs at bedtime. Does your child:

____ Refuse to go to bed on time.

____ Get out of bed many times.

____ Argue about going to bed.

____ Refuse to go to sleep unless someone sits with him or her.

____ Refuse to sleep in own bed.

____ Cry for attention.

____ Call out for parents.

____ Other _____

2. Take Action

The key to solving bedtime problems is to develop a routine and **stick to it**. It is also helpful to separate "sleeptime" from "bedtime." You cannot force your child to fall asleep, but you can insist that he or she be in bed at a certain hour. Allow your child to read or play in bed for a while. Eventually he or she will grow tired and fall asleep. Here are some ideas for solving bedtime problems. Check off the ones you will try.

___ *Set a daily bedtime.

___ *Establish a routine prior to bedtime (bathing, washing, brushing teeth, storytime).

___ *Verbally warn your child that bedtime is approaching, or set a timer to ring when it's time for bed. ("Mark, you have 15 more minutes until bedtime.")

___ Allow wind-down time for your child to relax. Suggest an activity that is not too stimulating.

___ Spend "quiet time" with your child prior to bedtime. Read a book together, have a conversation, play a quiet game, or select poetry whose rhythm is soothing and relaxing.

___ Play soft music on a tape recorder or record player.

___ Place a cup of water by your child's bed.

___ Once your child is in his or her room, set a timer. Allow your child to play quietly until the bell rings; then he or she must get into bed.

___ Talk about an interesting event that your child can look forward to upon awakening the next day.

___ Teach your child to read a clock; then give your child the responsibility of knowing when to go to bed. This method also works well for young children who wake up very early in the morning. ("You can't wake up Mommy or Daddy until the clock says 7:00.")

___ Other _____

If the problem continues...

3. Develop an Assertive Discipline Plan

Once you've alleviated your child's fears, made him or her comfortable and tucked your child into bed, your evening should be your own. If your child is still creating a fuss, he or she may be testing you to see if you mean what you say. In such cases, you will have to develop an Assertive Discipline Plan for bedtime. Determine the **Rule**, **Consequence** and **Reward**, then fill out the **Contract** on the next page.

The Rule

What will be the new rule in your house? Your child will:

___ Go to bed on time.

___ Stay in bed.

___ Go to bed without arguing.

___ Go to sleep alone.

___ Sleep in his or her own bed.

___ Go to sleep without calling out to parents.

___ Other _____

The Consequence

Use one of the following consequences or choose your own. Your child will:

___ Go to bed earlier the next night.

___ Lose TV privileges the next day.

___ Lose weekend "late night" privileges.

___ Other _____

The Reward

How will you reward your child for following the rule? Your child may:

___ Earn a sticker on the BEDTIME CHART. (See page 75.)

___ Receive the BEDTIME AWARD. (See page 77.)

___ Go to bed later on a night of your choosing.

___ Hear an extra story.

___ Play a special game with you before bed.

___ Stay up and watch an extra TV program the next night.

___ Have special time with you the next day.

___ Other _____

Bedtime Contract

The new rule in our house will be:

_____

If _____
Child's Name

does not follow the rule,

_____
Consequence

If _____

does follow the rule,

_____
Reward

Date _____

Sweet Dreams

When I reach my goal of _____ stickers, I will earn _____.

Parents: Place a sticker on the chart whenever your child goes to bed according to the rules. Younger children earn the reward in a few days, older children in a week.

Bedtime Award

presented to

_____

for

_____

Date _____

Bedtime Award

is presented to

_____

for

_____

_____

Date

Chapter 8

**Behavior in the Market
(And Other Public Places)**

Behavior in the Market

Chapter Eight

Note: This chapter can be used to solve behavior problems in all public places (markets, restaurants, doctors' offices, department stores, banks.) We address the market in particular since this is a place that parents often take their children on a regular basis. If problems occur in other public places, use the space marked "other" to develop your plan.

When working on this problem, keep in mind the major reason for teaching your child to behave in the market and other public places.

Children must learn that there are appropriate standards of behavior not only in their home, but in public places as well.

1. Pinpoint the Problem

Identify the specific problem that occurs in the market. Does your child:

___ Whine or beg for certain foods or items. ("I want it!")

___ Climb out of the cart.

___ Run through the aisles.

___ Pull items from the shelves.

___ Throw a tantrum when not getting his or her way.

___ Fight with siblings.

___ Other _____

2. Take Action

You can best help your child act more appropriately in the market by stating the exact behavior you expect, then making the experience as interesting as possible. Here are some ideas. Which ones will you try?

___ ★ BEFORE you enter the market, tell your child exactly what behavior you expect.

___ ★ Prepare a shopping list ahead of time to make the trip as short as possible.

___ Use an adult's belt as a "safety belt" to restrain toddlers in the basket seat.

___ Let your child hold the shopping list and mark off each item as you find it.

___ Involve your child in planning the evening meal. Have him or her suggest the items you will need.

___ Give an older child a calculator to add up each item; then compare the totals at the check-out counter.

___ Bring along a snack.

___ Allow your child to select one favorite food to add to your list.

___ Hand a younger child nonbreakable items to drop into the cart as you pick them off the shelves.

___ Other _____

> Tip: Since your child's attention span may be very short when in public places, bring along an activity to pass idle moments.

3. Develop an Assertive Discipline Plan

If it becomes necessary to utilize an Assertive Discipline Plan, be sure to communicate the **Rule**, **Consequence** and **Reward** to your child BEFORE you enter the market (or other public place). In this way you are teaching your child to be responsible for his or her actions. Write your plan on the **Contract** on page 83.

The Rule

What will be the rule in the market? Your child will:

___ Refrain from asking you to buy items.

___ Stay seated in cart.

___ Walk, not run, through the aisles.

___ Keep hands off items on shelves.

___ Exhibit self control (no tantrums).

___ Refrain from fighting with siblings.

___ Other _____

If the problem continues...

The Consequence

Choose consequences you can carry out on the spot, or immediately after you return home. Your child will:

___ Be taken outside to sit in the car. (Leave the full cart with the manager.) Once in the car, you sit in the front, and the child sits in the back. Stay in the car 2 minutes for a 2-year-old, 3 minutes for a 3-year-old, etc. Do not talk to your child. When the time is up, remind your child of the rule, praise appropriate behavior in the car and return to the market.

___ Sit in the "crabby chair" or go to the bedroom upon returning home.

___ Lose the privilege of playing outside with friends upon returning home.

___ Lose the privilege of participating in a scheduled afternoon activity.

___ Other _____ .

> **Tip:** The most effective way to impress upon your child that you will not tolerate inappropriate behavior in public is to remove your child from the situation. In most cases you can wait outside until he or she calms down. However, if necessary, leave a basket full of groceries in the market or an unfinished meal in a restaurant and take your child home immediately. Such dramatic action on your part will demonstrate to your child that you really mean business.

The Reward

How will you reward your child for following the rule? Your child can:

___ Earn a sticker on the Market Chart. (See page 85.)

___ Receive an award. (See page 87.)

___ Select one item to buy.

___ Have change for the gumball machine.

___ Be taken to the park or to a friend's house after you have returned home and the groceries are put away.

___ Help put groceries away.

___ Select a treat from the groceries just purchased.

___ Other _____

Contract for the Market
(or Other Public Places)

The new rule will be:

_____

If _____

Child's Name

does not follow the rule,

_____

Consequence

If _____

does follow the rule,

_____

Reward

Date _____

You are a SUPER STAR!

When I reach my goal of _____ stickers,
I will earn _____
_____.

Parents: Place stickers on the chart when your child acts appropriately in public places. So that younger children earn the reward quickly, give them two or more stickers when they behave.

Applause! Applause!

This award is presented to

_____

for

_____

Date _____

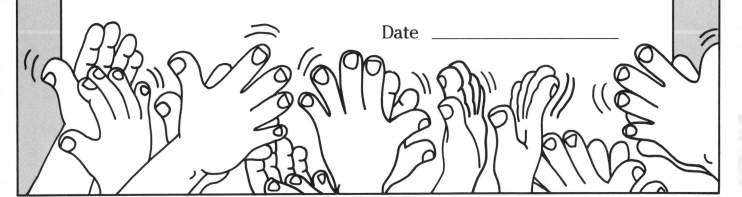

Applause! Applause!

This award is presented to

_____

for

_____

Date _____

Chapter 9

Behavior in the Car

Behavior in the Car

Chapter Nine

When working on this problem, keep in mind the two most important reasons why your child (and other young passengers) must learn to behave in the car:

For your safety, the children's safety, and that of the other cars on the road, you must have complete concentration while driving.

Aside from the safety factor, you have the right to drive without excess noise or distractions.

1. Pinpoint the Problem

Identify the specific problem that occurs in the car. Does your child (or the children in the carpool):

____ Fight or argue.

____ Talk too much.

____ Whine or cry.

____ Move around too much.

____ Play with the windows and/or locks.

____ Unbuckle the seat belt.

____ Play the radio too loudly.

____ Yell out the window.

____ Show off to other children.

____ Other _____

2. Take Action

Here are some ideas to help you prevent problems from arising in the car. The ideas cover trips with your child only as well as trips with other children. Check off the ones you will try:

___* Before the trip, discuss the rules of the car with your child (or the entire carpool). ("You will not fight or be noisy in this car.")

___* Insist that children wear seat belts. (Set a good example: you buckle up too.)

___ Place a barrier between children in the back seat (a box or suitcase) to designate "sides."

___ Assign seats.

___ Bring along a snack (raisins, pretzels, bagels, crackers).

___ Play tapes of children's stories or songs.

___ Bring along a favorite doll, stuffed animal, toy, game, magazine, catalog or book.

___ Keep a box in the trunk filled with activities and games. (Many toy companies make magnetic games especially designed for car use.)

___ Adjust the car seat or use a booster seat so that your child can see out of the window.

___ Have a sing-a-long.

___ Play games (count all the Volkswagons, red cars, station wagons; find out-of-state license plates; read billboards).

___ On long trips, take frequent breaks. Run, play tag, throw a ball.

___ Other _____

If the problem continues...

3. Develop an Assertive Discipline Plan

If problems continue, you must develop an Assertive Discipline Plan. Determine the **Rule**, **Consequence** and **Reward**; then fill out the **Contract** on page 93. Firmly communicate to all of your passengers the behaviors you expect of them. Inform the parents of the children in your carpool of your expectations as well.

The Rule

What will the rule be in your car? Your child (or the children in the carpool) will:

___ Ride without fighting or arguing.

___ Ride without whining or crying.

___ Sit still.

___ Keep the seat belt buckled.

___ Ride without yelling in the car or out the window.

___ Ride without touching the windows and/or locks.

___ Other _____

The Consequence

What will you do if your child (or the children in the carpool) continues to misbehave?

____ Pull over to the side, stop the car and wait until the fighting or noise subsides. Firmly and calmly state the behavior you expect. If the fighting or noise resumes when you're back on the road, pull over to the side again.

> **Tip:** Stopping the car is a very effective consequence, but you must be prepared to arrive late for an appointment, school or meeting. When children realize you are willing to be inconvenienced to teach them appropriate behavior, they will quickly learn you mean business.

____ Call the other children's parents to report on their misbehavior.

____ Keep a pad of paper near you or on the visor. Place a tick mark every time your child misbehaves. Each tick mark means 5 minutes earlier to bed that night or loss of a privilege.

____ Turn off the radio.

____ Send your child to his or her room the moment you return home.

____ Other _____

If the problem persists and presents a potential safety hazard, you must take severe action. Stop the car and say to your children: "If the two of you fight one more time, I will turn this car around, take both of you home, and you will both be grounded for the next 24 hours." Such an action may inconvenience you, your spouse or your children; however it will teach your children a vital lesson: that the family's safety in the car has more priority than anything else.

> **Remember:** Do not yell or become upset. Do not reach back to hit or grab a child. It is important that you remain calm, keep both hands on the wheel and stay in full control of the car in order to drive safely.

The Reward

How will you reward your child for appropriate car behavior?

Your child (or the children) may:

____ Earn a sticker on the CAR CHART. (See page 95.)

____ Be awarded the CAR AWARD. (See page 97.)

____ Select a favorite radio station.

____ Play a favorite cassette tape.

____ Eat a special snack as you drive.

____ Purchase a special treat or participate in a special activity upon arrival at the destination.

____ Other _____

Car Contract

The new rule in our house will be:

_____

If _____
                    Child's Name

does not follow the rule,

_____
                    Consequence

If _____

does follow the rule,

_____
                    Reward

Date _____

GRAND PRIX

When I reach my goal of _____ stickers, I will earn _____.

Parents: When your child behaves in the car, place a sticker on the Grand Prix Chart. Younger children may advance more than one step on the chart in order to earn the reward quickly. When the finish line is reached, your child earns the reward.

Positively Perfect Passenger Award

presented to

_____

for

_____

Date _____

Terrific Passenger Award

presented to

_____

for

_____

Date _____

Chapter 10

Babysitters

Babysitters

Chapter Ten

When working on this problem, keep in mind the two most important reasons why your child must learn to behave with the babysitter:

▪ Your child must learn to listen to whomever you have placed in charge.

▪ You need to be able to feel confident when leaving your child that the standards of behavior in your home are closely maintained.

1. Pinpoint the Problem

Identify the specific problem that occurs when you're not at home. Does your child:

___ Ignore the sitter's directions.

___ Stay up past bedtime.

___ Eat too much junk food.

___ Make a mess in the house.

___ Play wildly.

___ Fight with siblings.

___ Act disrespectful.

___ Leave the yard or stray away from the house.

___ Other _____

2. Take Action

Have a discussion with your child to determine the reasons why he or she doesn't behave with the babysitter; then do your best to eliminate any conditions that may be causing the problem. Here are some ideas. Check off the ones you will try.

___*In the babysitter's presence, communicate your expectations to your child. ("You will go to bed when the babysitter tells you to!")

___*In your child's presence, tell the sitter how you expect your child to behave, and that you want a report when you return home. Include special bedtime routines and the time your child should be in bed.

___ Plan something special for your child to do with the sitter (rent a video, bring out a special puzzle or game, set up a popcorn machine).

___ Encourage the sitter to read, color, paint, or do some activity with your child.

___ In the sitter's presence, tell your child which foods may and may not be eaten.

___ If you're planning to be away the whole day, leave a written schedule including activities, meals, TV time, bedtime, naptime.

___ Have the sitter vary the activities (go to the park, walk to the store).

___ Set out pajamas and make the room ready for bedtime before you leave the house.

___ Call your child just before bedtime to say goodnight.

___ Change babysitters if the situation warrants it.

___ Other _____

3. Develop an Assertive Discipline Plan

If the problem persists, develop a plan that includes the **Rule**, **Consequence** and **Reward**. Write your plan on the **Contract** on page 103. Decide beforehand who will provide the consequence - you or the sitter. If you choose to have the sitter discipline your child, leave specific instructions, and be sure to explain the extent of the sitter's authority in your child's presence. If you would prefer following through on your own, ask the sitter to monitor your child's behavior. When you return home, don't forget to be consistent and do what you said you would. In either case, inform both the sitter and your child of your plan.

> Tip: If your child continues to present a problem when you're not home, call at random intervals. If necessary, return home unexpectedly. Such drastic action will show your child that you really mean business.

If the problem continues...

The Rule

What will be the new rule in your house? Your child will:

____ Follow the babysitter's directions. ____ Get along with brothers and sisters.

____ Go to bed at the specified time. ____ Be respectful of the babysitter.

____ Eat only the permissible food. ____ Stay within specified boundaries.

____ Clean up before bedtime. ____ Other _____

____ Play calmly.

The Consequence

Decide whether you or the sitter will provide the consequence; then choose one of the following or use your own. Your child will:

____ Be sent to his or her room. ____ Stay in his or her room the next time you go out.

____ Sit in the "crabby chair" for a specified time. ____ Lose the privilege of having friends over when the sitter is there.

____ Lose favorite TV program privileges. ____ Other _____

____ Lose the privilege of playing with friends after school.

The Reward

As with the **Consequence**, you have the option of having the babysitter provide the **Reward** or doing so yourself when you return.

> **Tip:** An excellent way of encouraging children to behave well with a sitter is to use a "double reward" system; that is, the sitter gives the child a reward, then you provide a bonus reward later on.

How will you (or the sitter) reward your child for following the rule. Your child may:

____ Earn a sticker on the BABYSITTER CHART. (See page 105.)

____ Be awarded the BABYSITTER AWARD. (See page 107.)

____ Be given a special treat or small present from the sitter.

____ Stay up late that night or on a night of your choosing.

____ Be read an extra story at bedtime by the sitter.

____ Be taken to a special place the next day.

____ Have his or her favorite meal the next night.

____ Have a friend over the next time you go out.

____ Other _____

Babysitter Contract

The new rule in our house will be:

_____

If _____
Child's Name

does not follow the rule,

_____
Consequence

If _____

does follow the rule,

_____
Reward

Date _____

GOLD
MEDAL CHART

When I reach my goal of _____ stickers,
I will earn _____.

Parents: The goal will be determined by how often your child stays with the babysitter. Your child may earn the reward after behaving one time with the babysitter, or your child may have to earn more stickers if you use frequent child care.

Gold Medal for Cooperation

This award is presented to

_____

for

_____

Date _____

"Hip Hip Hooray"

This award is presented to

_____

for

_____

Date _____

Glossary of Terms

The following terms are used within the context of the Assertive Discipline program.

Assertive Discipline A step-by-step approach for teaching your child how to behave appropriately. To achieve success, you must have a take-charge attitude, a firm and calm way of communicating to your child, and a predetermined Assertive Discipline Plan.

Assertive Discipline Plan A three-part system for dealing with behavior problems - a rule, a consequence, a reward. An Assertive Discipline Plan should be communicated to your child as a choice: "If you choose not to follow the rule, there will be a consequence for your action. If you choose to follow the rule, there will be a reward."

Award A certificate to present to your child for behaving appropriately. An award should include your child's name and the reason that the award is being presented. To have the greatest effect, an award should be posted in a prominent place at home. Awards can also be framed and saved. **Note:** Do not confuse award with reward (see page 110).

Consequence As part of the Assertive Discipline Plan, a consequence naturally or logically results from a child's misbehavior. A consequence should be something your child does not like, but is in no way physically or psychologically harmful. The most common consequence used by parents is grounding the child in his or her room for a period of time without TV, radio, stereo or toys.

Consistency Essential for the success of your Discipline Plan, consistency means first saying you will provide a consequence, then following through and doing as you said you would. Consistency means reacting the same way each time to your child's behavior. Consistency also means agreement between spouses to support each other's method of discipline.

Contract The Assertive Discipline Plan in writing. A contract is a piece of paper that states the new rule in your home, the consequence that will occur if your child does not follow the rule, and the reward that your child will earn for behaving appropriately.

"Crabby" Chair Though called "crabby" chair, this consequence refers to "time out" in a chair or in any location in your home where a child who is misbehaving can be isolated for a specific period of time. For a younger child, place a chair within your view off to the side of the room. An older child can be sent to any unexciting place in the house where he or she can remain until the indicated time is up. The child is isolated for one minute for each year of age (five minutes for a five year old, nine minutes for a nine year old.)

Expectation The standard of behavior that you require of your child at home, in school, or in public places. Expectations should be clearly communicated so that your child knows exactly how you want him or her to behave.

Marble Mania An alternate method to the Positive Chart for tracking appropriate behavior. When your child follows the rule, praise him or her, then drop a marble into a glass jar. ("Chris, I'm so proud of the way you asked for my help without whining. You've earned a marble.") When the jar is filled (or you've reached a predetermined number of marbles) your child earns a reward. If your child spends an entire day without breaking a rule, drop bonus marbles into the jar. Marble Mania is an excellent way to encourage siblings to behave.

Positive Chart A method for tracking appropriate behavior. Determine a goal that your child can work towards, then place stickers on the chart whenever your child follows your rule. When the predetermined number of stickers has been reached, the child earns the reward or award that he or she has been working towards.

Positive Reinforcement The acknowledgement of appropriate behavior in the form of praise, hugs, kisses, smiles, rewards and awards. For behavior to change, you **must** positively reinforce your child frequently.

Reward Part of the Assertive Discipline Plan that acknowledges your child's appropriate behavior. A reward can be a privilege (staying up late), an activity (going to the movies), a gift (a new toy), an award (see page 109 for explanation). Use the Positive Charts in each chapter to determine when your child earns the reward. ("When you get 7 stickers on the Bedtime Chart you will earn a trip to the zoo.")

Rule Part of the Assertive Discipline Plan that states the behavior you expect from your child. The rule you establish should be very specific and communicated to your child in a clear and firm manner.

Special Time A reward for appropriate behavior. Special time is a period you set aside to do something with your child. The activity might be playing a favorite game, going to a movie, shopping, reading together, participating in a sport. The special time should be one-on-one without interruptions from other siblings.

Materials available from Lee Canter & Associates

Assertive Discipline for Parents Workshops and Homework Without Tears for Parents Workshops can be presented to your school or parenting group. Workshops and college courses on Assertive Discipline techniques are also available for educators.

For information or to order a catalog, write:

Lee Canter & Associates
P.O. Box 2113
Santa Monica, CA 90407-2113

Or call toll-free **(800) 262-4347**.

CA1009	Assertive Discipline for Parents
CA1010	Assertive Discipline Parent Resource Guide
CA1205	Homework Without Tears – Parent Guide
CA1223	Homework Organizer for Students

Effective Parenting Books

CA2053	Managing the Morning Rush
CA2054	Winning the Chores Wars
CA2055	Help! It's Homework Time
CA2056	Couch Potato Kids
CA2057	Surviving Sibling Rivalry
CA2058	No More Bedtime Battles
CA2059	What To Do When Your Child Needs To Study
CA2060	What To Do When Your Child Hates To Read
CA2061	What To Do When Your Child Won't Behave

Order from your local school supply dealer.